Eat When You're Hungry

Personal Food Journal

For Weight Loss

Based on the Hunger Scale

4 month food diary

Name _____

Start Date _____ End Date _____

Victoria K. Logan

Independently published

Table of Contents

Hunger Scale

Most people should eat when they reach **3** and stop when they reach **6**. This takes practice and isn't always possible. Try it at least once a day to start. Don't expect perfection.

1. EXTREME HUNGER: Possible symptoms: headache, difficulty concentrating, dizzy, trouble with coordination, complete lack of energy and a need to lie down. Some of these symptoms may occur during a very restrictive diet.

2. Irritable, cranky, lack energy, famished and possibly nauseous.

3. Need to eat. Empty feeling in stomach.

4. Starting to think about food. A little hungry.

5. Fueled enough to keep going. Physically and psychologically starting to feel satisfied.

6. Hunger is fully satisfied. You are lightly full.

7. More than satisfied. You're full but you can still eat.

8. Your stomach is starting to hurt. You ate more because it tasted good or because you were engaged in food-centered activity.

9. You feel uncomfortable, heavy, tired, and bloated.

10. EXTREME FULLNESS: You may have experienced this after Thanksgiving dinner. You are physically miserable and feel like you never want to look at food again.

For more information read
The Eat When You're Hungry Manifesto
by Victoria Logan on Amazon.com.

Introduction

Who this journal is for

This journal is for those who don't eat on a set schedule, who eat several small meals a day and/or for those who want to rate their hunger to practice eating when they're hungry and stopping when they're full.

Why use a daily food journal?

It has been shown that people who keep a daily food journal lose weight twice as fast as those who don't track their eating. If you're serious about losing weight you will benefit greatly from tracking your food intake.

Why rate hunger?

Our hunger drive was designed by nature to keep us alive. Without it we might forget to eat altogether. That's why our hunger drive becomes stronger the longer we go without food. We can't control hunger as so many diets tell us to do. But we can use this natural signal to fuel our body when it tells us to eat, and just as importantly, to stop when we're lightly full. It comes down to awareness.

Many people never get to the point of feeling even a little hunger. We eat because we're used to eating at the same time every day, it's "meal time", we smell food, or because others are eating. If weight loss is your goal it's good to notice these triggers and whether they are causing you to eat more than necessary.

To eat mindfully we can use hunger as an indicator that it's time to eat and time to stop. Don't let yourself be hungry for very long, unless you're experimenting. In addition, don't expect perfection, especially if you're new at this. Like all good things, being mindful of your hunger drive takes conitunual practice. To keep motivated give yourself a little reward when you follow through.

On a scale of 1 to 10, (see page 4), rate your level of hunger when you eat, even if you're not hungry at all. It's a way to analyze your habits. The key to success is to have something healthy ready to eat when you do get hungry. You don't need to wait until you're very hungry before every meal. Just practice!

Sample food diary

Date 5-20-16		M T W TH (F) S SU	Water ⊠ ⊠ ⊠ ⊠ ⊠ ⊠ ⊠ ⊠	
Time	**Hunger rating before 1-10**	**FOOD**	**Hunger rating after 1-10**	**Calories**
11 am	3	3/4 cup dry oatmeal	6	225
		1 T. raisins / 1 tsp. brown sugar		45
		1/2 c. almond milk		30
		sub total		300
2 pm	4	2 slices whole grain bread	5	200
		1/4 avocado and other veggies		60
		2 T. hummus		90
		100 calorie pack pretzels		100
		sub total		450
6 pm	3	1 cup rice	6	215
		1/2 c. beans		125
		1/4 avocado		60
		salsa, lettuce, onion		0
		2 olives (plus carrot, peppers, etc.)		15
		1/2 serving hummus		45
		sub total		460
10 am	2	apple	4	125
7 pm	1	two small cookies	3	165
		sub total		290

Hunger scale: most people should try for a 3 before they eat and stop eating at 6.	**Total Calories**	1500

What I did today. What I need to improve. Actions I will take tomorrow.
Packed a healthy lunch for work. Planned food for the day.

Drove to work. Start walking to work!

Exercise walking _____ Duration 30 min _____ Calories Burned 130

Sleep Time to bed 10:00 PM Wake up 5:10 am Hrs. 7 Min. 10

Weight & Measurements

Beginning

STARTING WEIGHT

bicep_____ chest/bust_____

waist_____ hips_____

thigh_____

1st Month

LOST

WEIGHT

bicep_____ chest/bust_____

waist_____ hips_____

thigh_____ **Inches lost**_____

2nd Month

LOST

WEIGHT

bicep_____ chest/bust_____

waist_____ hips_____

thigh_____ **Inches lost**_____

3rd Month

LOST

WEIGHT

bicep_____ chest/bust_____

waist_____ hips_____

thigh_____ **Inches lost**_____

4th Month

LOST

WEIGHT

bicep_____ chest/bust_____

waist_____ hips_____

thigh_____ **Inches lost**_____

5th Month

LOST

WEIGHT

bicep_____ chest/bust_____

waist_____ hips_____

thigh_____ **Inches lost**_____

6th Month

LOST

WEIGHT

bicep_____ chest/bust_____

waist_____ hips_____

thigh_____ **Inches lost**_____

TOTAL WEIGHT LOST [_____]   TOTAL INCHES LOST [_____]

Date		M T W TH F S SU	Water ○ ○ ○ ○ ○ ○ ○

Time	Hunger rating before 1-10	FOOD	Hunger rating after 1-10	Calories

Hunger scale: most people should try for a 3 before they eat and stop eating at 6.

Total Calories ⬚

What I did today. What I need to improve. Actions I will take tomorrow.

Exercise _____ Duration _____ Calories Burned _____

Sleep   Time to bed _____ Wake up _____ Hrs. _____ Min. _____

9

Date			M T W TH F S SU **Water** ○ ○ ○ ○ ○ ○ ○ ○		
Time	Hunger rating before 1-10	**FOOD**	Hunger rating after 1-10	**Calories**

Hunger scale: most people should try for a 3 before they eat and stop eating at 6.

Total Calories ⟨   ⟩

What I did today. What I need to improve. Actions I will take tomorrow.

Exercise _____ Duration _____ Calories Burned _____

Sleep Time to bed _____ Wake up _____ Hrs. _____ Min. _____

Date		M T W TH F S SU	Water ○ ○ ○ ○ ○ ○ ○ ○		
Time	Hunger rating before 1-10	FOOD	Hunger rating after 1-10	Calories

Hunger scale: most people should try for a 3 before they eat and stop eating at 6.

Total Calories ( )

What I did today. What I need to improve. Actions I will take tomorrow.

Exercise _____ Duration _____ Calories Burned _____

Sleep   Time to bed _____ Wake up _____ Hrs. _____ Min. _____

Time	Hunger rating before 1-10	FOOD	Hunger rating after 1-10	Calories
Date		M T W TH F S SU **Water** ○ ○ ○ ○ ○ ○ ○		

Hunger scale: most people should try for a 3 before they eat and stop eating at 6.

Total Calories ( )

What I did today. What I need to improve. Actions I will take tomorrow.

Exercise _____ Duration _____ Calories Burned _____

Sleep   Time to bed _____   Wake up _____   Hrs. _____   Min. _____

Date			M T W TH F S SU	Water ○ ○ ○ ○ ○ ○ ○		
Time	Hunger rating before 1-10		FOOD		Hunger rating after 1-10	Calories

Hunger scale: most people should try for a 3 before they eat and stop eating at 6.

Total Calories [   ]

What I did today. What I need to improve. Actions I will take tomorrow.

Exercise _____ Duration _____ Calories Burned _____

Sleep   Time to bed _____ Wake up _____ Hrs. _____ Min. _____

Date		M T W TH F S SU	Water ◯ ◯ ◯ ◯ ◯ ◯ ◯ ◯	
Time	Hunger rating before 1-10	FOOD	Hunger rating after 1-10	Calories

Hunger scale: most people should try for a 3 before they eat and stop eating at 6.

Total Calories ⬚

What I did today. What I need to improve. Actions I will take tomorrow.

Exercise _____ Duration _____ Calories Burned _____

Sleep   Time to bed _____   Wake up _____   Hrs. _____   Min. _____

Date			M T W TH F S SU	Water ○ ○ ○ ○ ○ ○ ○ ○	
Time	**Hunger rating before 1-10**	**FOOD**		**Hunger rating after 1-10**	**Calories**

Hunger scale: most people should try for a 3 before they eat and stop eating at 6.

Total Calories ⬭

What I did today. What I need to improve. Actions I will take tomorrow.

Exercise _____ Duration _____ Calories Burned _____

Sleep   Time to bed _____ Wake up _____ Hrs. _____ Min. _____

15

Date		M T W TH F S SU	Water ○ ○ ○ ○ ○ ○ ○ ○		
Time	Hunger rating before 1-10	**FOOD**		Hunger rating after 1-10	**Calories**

Hunger scale: most people should try for a 3 before they eat and stop eating at 6.

Total Calories (_____)

What I did today. What I need to improve. Actions I will take tomorrow.

Exercise _____ Duration _____ Calories Burned _____

Sleep   Time to bed _____   Wake up _____   Hrs. _____   Min. _____

Date		M T W TH F S SU	Water ○ ○ ○ ○ ○ ○ ○ ○		
Time	Hunger rating before 1-10	FOOD	Hunger rating after 1-10	Calories

Hunger scale: most people should try for a 3 before they eat and stop eating at 6.

Total Calories

What I did today. What I need to improve. Actions I will take tomorrow.

Exercise _____ Duration _____ Calories Burned _____

Sleep Time to bed _____ Wake up _____ Hrs. _____ Min. _____

Date		M T W TH F S SU	Water ◯ ◯ ◯ ◯ ◯ ◯ ◯ ◯	
Time	Hunger rating before 1-10	**FOOD**	Hunger rating after 1-10	**Calories**

Hunger scale: most people should try for a 3 before they eat and stop eating at 6.

Total Calories ⟨_____⟩

What I did today. What I need to improve. Actions I will take tomorrow.

Exercise _____ Duration _____ Calories Burned _____

Sleep   Time to bed _____ Wake up _____ Hrs. _____ Min. _____

Date		M T W TH F S SU	Water ○ ○ ○ ○ ○ ○ ○		
Time	Hunger rating before 1-10	FOOD	Hunger rating after 1-10	Calories

Hunger scale: most people should try for a 3 before they eat and stop eating at 6.

Total Calories [   ]

What I did today. What I need to improve. Actions I will take tomorrow.

_____

_____

_____

Exercise _____ Duration _____ Calories Burned _____

Sleep   Time to bed _____ Wake up _____ Hrs. _____ Min. _____

Date		M T W TH F S SU	Water ◯ ◯ ◯ ◯ ◯ ◯ ◯ ◯	
Time	Hunger rating before 1-10	**FOOD**	Hunger rating after 1-10	**Calories**

Hunger scale: most people should try for a 3 before they eat and stop eating at 6.

Total Calories ( )

What I did today. What I need to improve. Actions I will take tomorrow.

Exercise _____ Duration _____ Calories Burned _____

Sleep   Time to bed _____   Wake up _____   Hrs. _____   Min. _____

Date		M T W TH F S SU	Water ○ ○ ○ ○ ○ ○ ○		
Time	Hunger rating before 1-10	**FOOD**		Hunger rating after 1-10	**Calories**

Hunger scale: most people should try for a 3 before they eat and stop eating at 6.

Total Calories ( )

What I did today. What I need to improve. Actions I will take tomorrow.

Exercise _____ Duration _____ Calories Burned _____

Sleep Time to bed _____ Wake up _____ Hrs. _____ Min. _____

21

Date			M T W TH F S SU Water ○ ○ ○ ○ ○ ○ ○		
Time	Hunger rating before 1-10	FOOD	Hunger rating after 1-10	Calories

Hunger scale: most people should try for a 3 before they eat and stop eating at 6.

Total Calories ( )

What I did today. What I need to improve. Actions I will take tomorrow.

Exercise _____ Duration _____ Calories Burned _____

Sleep   Time to bed _____ Wake up _____ Hrs. _____ Min. _____

Date		M T W TH F S SU	Water ○ ○ ○ ○ ○ ○ ○		
Time	Hunger rating before 1-10	FOOD		Hunger rating after 1-10	Calories

Hunger scale: most people should try for a 3 before they eat and stop eating at 6.

Total Calories ( )

What I did today. What I need to improve. Actions I will take tomorrow.

Exercise _____ Duration _____ Calories Burned _____

Sleep Time to bed _____ Wake up _____ Hrs. _____ Min._____

Date		M T W TH F S SU	Water ○ ○ ○ ○ ○ ○ ○ ○	
Time	Hunger rating before 1-10	**FOOD**	Hunger rating after 1-10	**Calories**

Hunger scale: most people should try for a 3 before they eat and stop eating at 6.

Total Calories ⬭

What I did today. What I need to improve. Actions I will take tomorrow.

Exercise _____ Duration _____ Calories Burned _____

Sleep Time to bed _____ Wake up _____ Hrs. _____ Min. _____

Date		M T W TH F S SU	**Water** ○ ○ ○ ○ ○ ○ ○		
Time	Hunger rating before 1-10	**FOOD**	Hunger rating after 1-10	**Calories**

Hunger scale: most people should try for a 3 before they eat and stop eating at 6.   **Total Calories** ⌷

What I did today. What I need to improve. Actions I will take tomorrow.

Exercise _____ Duration _____ Calories Burned _____

Sleep   Time to bed _____   Wake up _____   Hrs. _____   Min. _____

Date			M T W TH F S SU	Water ○ ○ ○ ○ ○ ○ ○ ○	
Time	Hunger rating before 1-10	**FOOD**		Hunger rating after 1-10	**Calories**

Hunger scale: most people should try for a 3 before they eat and stop eating at 6.

Total Calories ( )

What I did today. What I need to improve. Actions I will take tomorrow.

Exercise _____ Duration _____ Calories Burned _____

Sleep Time to bed _____ Wake up _____ Hrs. _____ Min. _____

Date		M T W TH F S SU	Water ○ ○ ○ ○ ○ ○ ○ ○		
Time	Hunger rating before 1-10	**FOOD**		Hunger rating after 1-10	**Calories**

Hunger scale: most people should try for a 3 before they eat and stop eating at 6.

Total Calories ( )

What I did today. What I need to improve. Actions I will take tomorrow.

Exercise _____ Duration _____ Calories Burned _____

Sleep   Time to bed _____ Wake up _____ Hrs. _____ Min. _____

Date		M T W TH F S SU	Water ○ ○ ○ ○ ○ ○ ○	
Time	Hunger rating before 1-10	**FOOD**	Hunger rating after 1-10	**Calories**

Hunger scale: most people should try for a 3 before they eat and stop eating at 6.

Total Calories ( )

What I did today. What I need to improve. Actions I will take tomorrow.

Exercise _____ Duration _____ Calories Burned _____

Sleep   Time to bed _____   Wake up _____   Hrs. _____   Min. _____

Date		M T W TH F S SU	**Water** ○ ○ ○ ○ ○ ○ ○ ○		
Time	Hunger rating before 1-10	**FOOD**		Hunger rating after 1-10	**Calories**

Hunger scale: most people should try for a 3 before they eat and stop eating at 6.

Total Calories [   ]

What I did today. What I need to improve. Actions I will take tomorrow.

Exercise _____ Duration _____ Calories Burned _____

Sleep   Time to bed _____ Wake up _____ Hrs. _____ Min. _____

Time	Hunger rating before 1-10	FOOD	Hunger rating after 1-10	Calories
Date		M T W TH F S SU Water ○ ○ ○ ○ ○ ○ ○		

Hunger scale: most people should try for a 3 before they eat and stop eating at 6.

Total Calories ⬭

What I did today. What I need to improve. Actions I will take tomorrow.

Exercise _____ Duration _____ Calories Burned _____

Sleep   Time to bed _____ Wake up _____ Hrs. _____ Min._____

Date		M T W TH F S SU	Water ○ ○ ○ ○ ○ ○ ○		
Time	Hunger rating before 1-10	FOOD		Hunger rating after 1-10	Calories

Hunger scale: most people should try for a 3 before they eat and stop eating at 6.

Total Calories [   ]

What I did today. What I need to improve. Actions I will take tomorrow.

Exercise _____ Duration _____ Calories Burned _____

Sleep   Time to bed _____ Wake up _____ Hrs. _____ Min. _____

Date		M T W TH F S SU	Water ○ ○ ○ ○ ○ ○ ○ ○		
Time	Hunger rating before 1-10	**FOOD**		Hunger rating after 1-10	**Calories**

Hunger scale: most people should try for a 3 before they eat and stop eating at 6.

Total Calories ( )

What I did today. What I need to improve. Actions I will take tomorrow.

Exercise _____ Duration _____ Calories Burned _____

Sleep   Time to bed _____ Wake up _____ Hrs. _____ Min. _____

Date		M T W TH F S SU	Water ○ ○ ○ ○ ○ ○ ○ ○		
Time	Hunger rating before 1-10	**FOOD**		Hunger rating after 1-10	Calories

Hunger scale: most people should try for a 3 before they eat and stop eating at 6.

Total Calories ⬭

What I did today. What I need to improve. Actions I will take tomorrow.

Exercise _____ Duration _____ Calories Burned _____

Sleep Time to bed _____ Wake up _____ Hrs. _____ Min. _____

Date		M T W TH F S SU	Water ◯ ◯ ◯ ◯ ◯ ◯ ◯		
Time	Hunger rating before 1-10	FOOD		Hunger rating after 1-10	Calories

Hunger scale: most people should try for a 3 before they eat and stop eating at 6.

Total Calories ⎛_____⎞

What I did today. What I need to improve. Actions I will take tomorrow.

Exercise _____ Duration _____ Calories Burned _____

Sleep Time to bed _____ Wake up _____ Hrs. _____ Min. _____

Date			M T W TH F S SU	Water ◯ ◯ ◯ ◯ ◯ ◯ ◯ ◯	
Time	Hunger rating before 1-10	**FOOD**		Hunger rating after 1-10	Calories

Hunger scale: most people should try for a 3 before they eat and stop eating at 6.

Total Calories ⬭

What I did today. What I need to improve. Actions I will take tomorrow.

Exercise _____ Duration _____ Calories Burned _____

Sleep Time to bed _____ Wake up _____ Hrs. _____ Min. _____

Date			M T W TH F S SU	Water ○ ○ ○ ○ ○ ○ ○ ○	
Time	Hunger rating before 1-10	**FOOD**		Hunger rating after 1-10	**Calories**

Hunger scale: most people should try for a 3 before they eat and stop eating at 6.

Total Calories ( )

What I did today. What I need to improve. Actions I will take tomorrow.

Exercise _____ Duration _____ Calories Burned _____

Sleep Time to bed _____ Wake up _____ Hrs. _____ Min. _____

Date		M T W TH F S SU	Water ○ ○ ○ ○ ○ ○ ○	
Time	Hunger rating before 1-10	FOOD	Hunger rating after 1-10	Calories

Hunger scale: most people should try for a 3 before they eat and stop eating at 6.

Total Calories [   ]

What I did today. What I need to improve. Actions I will take tomorrow.

Exercise _____ Duration _____ Calories Burned _____

Sleep   Time to bed _____ Wake up _____ Hrs. _____ Min. _____

Date		M T W TH F S SU	Water ◯ ◯ ◯ ◯ ◯ ◯ ◯		
Time	Hunger rating before 1-10	FOOD	Hunger rating after 1-10	Calories

Hunger scale: most people should try for a 3 before they eat and stop eating at 6.

Total Calories

What I did today. What I need to improve. Actions I will take tomorrow.

Exercise _____ Duration _____ Calories Burned _____

Sleep   Time to bed _____   Wake up _____   Hrs. _____   Min. _____

Date		M T W TH F S SU	Water ○ ○ ○ ○ ○ ○ ○ ○	
Time	Hunger rating before **1-10**	**FOOD**	Hunger rating after **1-10**	**Calories**

Hunger scale: most people should try for a 3 before they eat and stop eating at 6.

Total Calories ⬭

What I did today. What I need to improve. Actions I will take tomorrow.

Exercise _____ Duration _____ Calories Burned _____

Sleep   Time to bed _____   Wake up _____   Hrs. _____   Min. _____

1st Monthly Check-in

Date		M T W TH F S SU	Water ○ ○ ○ ○ ○ ○ ○ ○		
Time	Hunger rating before 1-10	FOOD		Hunger rating after 1-10	Calories

Hunger scale: most people should try for a 3 before they eat and stop eating at 6.

Total Calories ( )

What I did today. What I need to improve. Actions I will take tomorrow.

_____

_____

Exercise _____ Duration _____ Calories Burned _____

Sleep Time to bed _____ Wake up _____ Hrs. _____ Min. _____

Date		M T W TH F S SU	Water ◯ ◯ ◯ ◯ ◯ ◯ ◯ ◯		
Time	Hunger rating before 1-10	**FOOD**		Hunger rating after 1-10	**Calories**

Hunger scale: most people should try for a 3 before they eat and stop eating at 6.

Total Calories ◯

What I did today. What I need to improve. Actions I will take tomorrow.

Exercise _____ Duration _____ Calories Burned _____

Sleep   Time to bed _____   Wake up _____   Hrs. _____   Min._____

Date		M T W TH F S SU	Water ◯ ◯ ◯ ◯ ◯ ◯ ◯ ◯	
Time	Hunger rating before 1-10	FOOD	Hunger rating after 1-10	Calories

Hunger scale: most people should try for a 3 before they eat and stop eating at 6.

Total Calories

What I did today. What I need to improve. Actions I will take tomorrow.

Exercise _____ Duration _____ Calories Burned _____

Sleep Time to bed _____ Wake up _____ Hrs. _____ Min. _____

43

Date		M T W TH F S SU	Water ○ ○ ○ ○ ○ ○ ○ ○		
Time	Hunger rating before 1-10	**FOOD**		Hunger rating after 1-10	**Calories**

Hunger scale: most people should try for a 3 before they eat and stop eating at 6.

Total Calories ( )

What I did today. What I need to improve. Actions I will take tomorrow.

Exercise _____ Duration _____ Calories Burned _____

Sleep Time to bed _____ Wake up _____ Hrs. _____ Min. _____

Date		M T W TH F S SU	Water ○ ○ ○ ○ ○ ○ ○ ○	
Time	Hunger rating before 1-10	**FOOD**	Hunger rating after 1-10	**Calories**

Hunger scale: most people should try for a 3 before they eat and stop eating at 6.

Total Calories ⬭

What I did today. What I need to improve. Actions I will take tomorrow.

Exercise _____ Duration _____ Calories Burned _____

Sleep   Time to bed _____   Wake up _____   Hrs. _____   Min. _____

Date		M T W TH F S SU	Water ◯ ◯ ◯ ◯ ◯ ◯ ◯		
Time	Hunger rating before 1-10	**FOOD**	Hunger rating after 1-10	**Calories**

Hunger scale: most people should try for a 3 before they eat and stop eating at 6.

Total Calories ⬭

What I did today. What I need to improve. Actions I will take tomorrow.

Exercise _____ Duration _____ Calories Burned _____

Sleep   Time to bed _____   Wake up _____   Hrs. _____   Min. _____

46

Date		M T W TH F S SU	Water ○ ○ ○ ○ ○ ○ ○	
Time	Hunger rating before 1-10	FOOD	Hunger rating after 1-10	Calories

Hunger scale: most people should try for a 3 before they eat and stop eating at 6.

Total Calories ( )

What I did today. What I need to improve. Actions I will take tomorrow.

Exercise _____ Duration _____ Calories Burned _____

Sleep   Time to bed _____   Wake up _____   Hrs. _____   Min. _____

Date		M T W TH F S SU	Water ○ ○ ○ ○ ○ ○ ○		
Time	Hunger rating before 1-10	**FOOD**	Hunger rating after 1-10	**Calories**

Hunger scale: most people should try for a 3 before they eat and stop eating at 6.

Total Calories (   )

What I did today. What I need to improve. Actions I will take tomorrow.

Exercise _____ Duration _____ Calories Burned _____

Sleep   Time to bed _____ Wake up _____ Hrs. _____ Min. _____

48

Date		M T W TH F S SU	Water $\bigcirc \bigcirc \bigcirc \bigcirc \bigcirc \bigcirc \bigcirc \bigcirc$		
Time	Hunger rating before 1-10	FOOD		Hunger rating after 1-10	Calories

Hunger scale: most people should try for a 3 before they eat and stop eating at 6.

Total Calories ( )

What I did today. What I need to improve. Actions I will take tomorrow.

Exercise _____ Duration _____ Calories Burned _____

Sleep   Time to bed _____ Wake up _____ Hrs. _____ Min. _____

Date		M T W TH F S SU	Water ○ ○ ○ ○ ○ ○ ○ ○		
Time	Hunger rating before 1-10	**FOOD**	Hunger rating after 1-10	**Calories**

Hunger scale: most people should try for a 3 before they eat and stop eating at 6.

Total Calories (   )

What I did today. What I need to improve. Actions I will take tomorrow.

Exercise _____ Duration _____ Calories Burned _____

Sleep   Time to bed _____ Wake up _____ Hrs. _____ Min. _____

Date		M T W TH F S SU **Water** ○ ○ ○ ○ ○ ○ ○ ○		
Time	Hunger rating before 1-10	**FOOD**	Hunger rating after 1-10	**Calories**

Hunger scale: most people should try for a 3 before they eat and stop eating at 6.

Total Calories ( )

What I did today. What I need to improve. Actions I will take tomorrow.

Exercise _____ Duration _____ Calories Burned _____

Sleep   Time to bed _____ Wake up _____ Hrs. _____ Min. _____

Date		M T W TH F S SU	Water ○ ○ ○ ○ ○ ○ ○	
Time	Hunger rating before 1-10	**FOOD**	Hunger rating after 1-10	**Calories**

Hunger scale: most people should try for a 3 before they eat and stop eating at 6.

Total Calories (   )

What I did today. What I need to improve. Actions I will take tomorrow.

Exercise _____ Duration _____ Calories Burned _____

Sleep Time to bed _____ Wake up _____ Hrs. _____ Min. _____

Date		M T W TH F S SU	Water ◯ ◯ ◯ ◯ ◯ ◯ ◯		
Time	Hunger rating before 1-10	**FOOD**	Hunger rating after 1-10	**Calories**

Hunger scale: most people should try for a 3 before they eat and stop eating at 6.

Total Calories [   ]

What I did today. What I need to improve. Actions I will take tomorrow.

_____

_____

_____

Exercise _____ Duration _____ Calories Burned _____

Sleep Time to bed _____ Wake up _____ Hrs. _____ Min. _____

Date			M T W TH F S SU	Water ◯ ◯ ◯ ◯ ◯ ◯ ◯	
Time	Hunger rating before 1-10	FOOD		Hunger rating after 1-10	Calories

Hunger scale: most people should try for a 3 before they eat and stop eating at 6.

Total Calories ⬭

What I did today. What I need to improve. Actions I will take tomorrow.

Exercise _____ Duration _____ Calories Burned _____

Sleep   Time to bed _____ Wake up _____ Hrs. _____ Min. _____

54

Date		M T W TH F S SU	Water ○ ○ ○ ○ ○ ○ ○ ○		
Time	Hunger rating before 1-10	FOOD	Hunger rating after 1-10	Calories

Hunger scale: most people should try for a 3 before they eat and stop eating at 6.

Total Calories ⟨   ⟩

What I did today. What I need to improve. Actions I will take tomorrow.

Exercise _____ Duration _____ Calories Burned _____

Sleep   Time to bed _____   Wake up _____   Hrs. _____   Min. _____

Date		M T W TH F S SU	Water ○ ○ ○ ○ ○ ○ ○	
Time	Hunger rating before 1-10	FOOD	Hunger rating after 1-10	Calories

Hunger scale: most people should try for a 3 before they eat and stop eating at 6.

Total Calories ⬭

What I did today. What I need to improve. Actions I will take tomorrow.
_____

Exercise _____ Duration _____ Calories Burned _____

Sleep   Time to bed _____   Wake up _____   Hrs. _____   Min. _____

56

Date			M T W TH F S SU	Water ○ ○ ○ ○ ○ ○ ○		
Time	Hunger rating before 1-10		FOOD	Hunger rating after 1-10	Calories

Hunger scale: most people should try for a 3 before they eat and stop eating at 6.

Total Calories ⬭

What I did today. What I need to improve. Actions I will take tomorrow.

Exercise _____ Duration _____ Calories Burned _____

Sleep Time to bed _____ Wake up _____ Hrs. _____ Min. _____

Date		M T W TH F S SU	Water ○ ○ ○ ○ ○ ○ ○ ○		
Time	Hunger rating before 1-10	**FOOD**	Hunger rating after 1-10	**Calories**

Hunger scale: most people should try for a 3 before they eat and stop eating at 6.

Total Calories ( )

What I did today. What I need to improve. Actions I will take tomorrow.

Exercise _____ Duration _____ Calories Burned _____

Sleep   Time to bed _____   Wake up _____   Hrs. _____   Min. _____

Date		M T W TH F S SU	Water ○ ○ ○ ○ ○ ○ ○ ○		
Time	Hunger rating before 1-10	FOOD	Hunger rating after 1-10	Calories

Hunger scale: most people should try for a 3 before they eat and stop eating at 6.

Total Calories ⌐   ⌐

What I did today. What I need to improve. Actions I will take tomorrow.

_____

_____

_____

Exercise _____ Duration _____ Calories Burned _____

Sleep   Time to bed _____ Wake up _____ Hrs. _____ Min. _____

Date		M T W TH F S SU	Water ○ ○ ○ ○ ○ ○ ○		
Time	Hunger rating before 1-10	**FOOD**		Hunger rating after 1-10	**Calories**

Hunger scale: most people should try for a 3 before they eat and stop eating at 6.

Total Calories

What I did today. What I need to improve. Actions I will take tomorrow.

Exercise _____ Duration _____ Calories Burned _____

Sleep   Time to bed _____   Wake up _____   Hrs. _____   Min. _____

Date		M T W TH F S SU	Water ○ ○ ○ ○ ○ ○ ○ ○	
Time	Hunger rating before 1-10	FOOD	Hunger rating after 1-10	Calories

Hunger scale: most people should try for a 3 before they eat and stop eating at 6.

Total Calories ( )

What I did today. What I need to improve. Actions I will take tomorrow.

Exercise _____ Duration _____ Calories Burned _____

Sleep   Time to bed _____ Wake up _____ Hrs. _____ Min. _____

Date		M T W TH F S SU	Water ○ ○ ○ ○ ○ ○ ○ ○	
Time	Hunger rating before 1-10	**FOOD**	Hunger rating after 1-10	**Calories**

Hunger scale: most people should try for a 3 before they eat and stop eating at 6.

Total Calories ⟨_____⟩

What I did today. What I need to improve. Actions I will take tomorrow.

Exercise _____ Duration _____ Calories Burned _____

Sleep Time to bed _____ Wake up _____ Hrs. _____ Min. _____

Date		M T W TH F S SU	Water ○ ○ ○ ○ ○ ○ ○	
Time	Hunger rating before 1-10	**FOOD**	Hunger rating after 1-10	**Calories**

Hunger scale: most people should try for a 3 before they eat and stop eating at 6.

Total Calories ( )

What I did today. What I need to improve. Actions I will take tomorrow.

Exercise _____ Duration _____ Calories Burned _____

Sleep Time to bed _____ Wake up _____ Hrs. _____ Min. _____

Date			M T W TH F S SU	Water ◯◯◯◯◯◯◯◯	
Time	Hunger rating before 1-10	**FOOD**		Hunger rating after 1-10	**Calories**

Hunger scale: most people should try for a 3 before they eat and stop eating at 6.

Total Calories ◯

What I did today. What I need to improve. Actions I will take tomorrow.

Exercise _____ Duration _____ Calories Burned _____

Sleep Time to bed _____ Wake up _____ Hrs. _____ Min. _____

Date		M T W TH F S SU	Water ○ ○ ○ ○ ○ ○ ○ ○		
Time	Hunger rating before 1-10	**FOOD**		Hunger rating after 1-10	**Calories**

Hunger scale: most people should try for a 3 before they eat and stop eating at 6.

Total Calories ⌁

What I did today. What I need to improve. Actions I will take tomorrow.

Exercise _____ Duration _____ Calories Burned _____

Sleep   Time to bed _____ Wake up _____ Hrs. _____ Min. _____

Date		M T W TH F S SU	Water ○ ○ ○ ○ ○ ○ ○ ○		
Time	Hunger rating before 1-10	**FOOD**	Hunger rating after 1-10	**Calories**

Hunger scale: most people should try for
a 3 before they eat and stop eating at 6.

Total Calories ( )

What I did today. What I need to improve. Actions I will take tomorrow.

Exercise _____ Duration _____ Calories Burned _____

Sleep   Time to bed _____   Wake up _____   Hrs. _____   Min. _____

Date		M T W TH F S SU	**Water** ○ ○ ○ ○ ○ ○ ○ ○		
Time	Hunger rating before 1-10	**FOOD**		Hunger rating after 1-10	**Calories**

Hunger scale: most people should try for a 3 before they eat and stop eating at 6.

Total Calories

What I did today. What I need to improve. Actions I will take tomorrow.

Exercise _____ Duration _____ Calories Burned _____

Sleep   Time to bed _____ Wake up _____ Hrs. _____ Min._____

Date		M T W TH F S SU	Water ◯ ◯ ◯ ◯ ◯ ◯ ◯	
Time	Hunger rating before 1-10	**FOOD**	Hunger rating after 1-10	**Calories**

Hunger scale: most people should try for a 3 before they eat and stop eating at 6.

Total Calories ◯

What I did today. What I need to improve. Actions I will take tomorrow.

Exercise _____ Duration _____ Calories Burned _____

Sleep Time to bed _____ Wake up _____ Hrs. _____ Min. _____

Date		M T W TH F S SU	Water ○ ○ ○ ○ ○ ○ ○	
Time	Hunger rating before 1-10	**FOOD**	Hunger rating after 1-10	**Calories**

Hunger scale: most people should try for a 3 before they eat and stop eating at 6.

Total Calories [ ]

What I did today. What I need to improve. Actions I will take tomorrow.

Exercise _____ Duration _____ Calories Burned _____

Sleep Time to bed _____ Wake up _____ Hrs. _____ Min. _____

Date		M T W TH F S SU	Water ○ ○ ○ ○ ○ ○ ○ ○	
Time	Hunger rating before 1-10	**FOOD**	Hunger rating after 1-10	**Calories**

Hunger scale: most people should try for a 3 before they eat and stop eating at 6.

Total Calories ( )

What I did today. What I need to improve. Actions I will take tomorrow.

Exercise _____ Duration _____ Calories Burned _____

Sleep   Time to bed _____   Wake up _____   Hrs. _____   Min. _____

70

Date			M T W TH F S SU Water ○ ○ ○ ○ ○ ○ ○ ○		
Time	Hunger rating before 1-10	**FOOD**	Hunger rating after 1-10	**Calories**

Hunger scale: most people should try for a 3 before they eat and stop eating at 6.

Total Calories ( )

What I did today. What I need to improve. Actions I will take tomorrow.

_____

_____

_____

Exercise _____ Duration _____ Calories Burned _____

Sleep Time to bed _____ Wake up _____ Hrs. _____ Min._____

2nd Monthly Check-in

Date		M T W TH F S SU	Water ◯ ◯ ◯ ◯ ◯ ◯ ◯ ◯		
Time	Hunger rating before 1-10	FOOD	Hunger rating after 1-10	Calories

Hunger scale: most people should try for a 3 before they eat and stop eating at 6.

Total Calories

What I did today. What I need to improve. Actions I will take tomorrow.

Exercise _____ Duration _____ Calories Burned _____

Sleep   Time to bed _____ Wake up _____ Hrs. _____ Min. _____

73

Date		M T W TH F S SU	Water ○ ○ ○ ○ ○ ○ ○ ○	
Time	Hunger rating before 1-10	**FOOD**	Hunger rating after 1-10	**Calories**

Hunger scale: most people should try for a 3 before they eat and stop eating at 6.

Total Calories ( )

What I did today. What I need to improve. Actions I will take tomorrow.

Exercise _____ Duration _____ Calories Burned _____

Sleep Time to bed _____ Wake up _____ Hrs. _____ Min. _____

Date		M T W TH F S SU	Water ○ ○ ○ ○ ○ ○ ○ ○	
Time	Hunger rating before 1-10	FOOD	Hunger rating after 1-10	Calories

Hunger scale: most people should try for a 3 before they eat and stop eating at 6.

Total Calories [   ]

What I did today. What I need to improve. Actions I will take tomorrow.

_____

_____

Exercise _____ Duration _____ Calories Burned _____

Sleep   Time to bed _____   Wake up _____   Hrs. _____   Min. _____

Date		M T W TH F S SU	Water ○ ○ ○ ○ ○ ○ ○ ○	
Time	Hunger rating before 1-10	**FOOD**	Hunger rating after 1-10	**Calories**

Hunger scale: most people should try for a 3 before they eat and stop eating at 6.

Total Calories ( )

What I did today. What I need to improve. Actions I will take tomorrow.

Exercise _____ Duration _____ Calories Burned _____

Sleep Time to bed _____ Wake up _____ Hrs. _____ Min. _____

Date		M T W TH F S SU	Water ○ ○ ○ ○ ○ ○ ○		
Time	Hunger rating before 1-10	FOOD	Hunger rating after 1-10	Calories

Hunger scale: most people should try for a 3 before they eat and stop eating at 6.

Total Calories ( )

What I did today. What I need to improve. Actions I will take tomorrow.

Exercise _____ Duration _____ Calories Burned _____

Sleep Time to bed _____ Wake up _____ Hrs. _____ Min. _____

Date		M T W TH F S SU	Water ○ ○ ○ ○ ○ ○ ○		
Time	Hunger rating before 1-10	**FOOD**	Hunger rating after 1-10	**Calories**

Hunger scale: most people should try for a 3 before they eat and stop eating at 6.

Total Calories ⬚

What I did today. What I need to improve. Actions I will take tomorrow.

Exercise _____ Duration _____ Calories Burned _____

Sleep   Time to bed _____ Wake up _____ Hrs. _____ Min. _____

Date		M T W TH F S SU **Water** ○ ○ ○ ○ ○ ○ ○ ○		
Time	Hunger rating before **1-10**	**FOOD**	Hunger rating after **1-10**	**Calories**

Hunger scale: most people should try for a 3 before they eat and stop eating at 6.

Total Calories

What I did today. What I need to improve. Actions I will take tomorrow.

Exercise _____ Duration _____ Calories Burned _____

Sleep   Time to bed _____ Wake up _____ Hrs. _____ Min. _____

Date		M T W TH F S SU	Water ○ ○ ○ ○ ○ ○ ○ ○

Time	Hunger rating before 1-10	FOOD	Hunger rating after 1-10	Calories

Hunger scale: most people should try for a 3 before they eat and stop eating at 6.

Total Calories ( )

What I did today. What I need to improve. Actions I will take tomorrow.

Exercise _____ Duration _____ Calories Burned _____

Sleep Time to bed _____ Wake up _____ Hrs. _____ Min. _____

Date		M T W TH F S SU	Water ○ ○ ○ ○ ○ ○ ○	
Time	Hunger rating before 1-10	FOOD	Hunger rating after 1-10	Calories

Hunger scale: most people should try for a 3 before they eat and stop eating at 6.

Total Calories ⬭

What I did today. What I need to improve. Actions I will take tomorrow.

Exercise _____ Duration _____ Calories Burned _____

Sleep   Time to bed _____ Wake up _____ Hrs. _____ Min. _____

81

Date		M T W TH F S SU	Water ○ ○ ○ ○ ○ ○ ○ ○		
Time	Hunger rating before 1-10	**FOOD**		Hunger rating after 1-10	**Calories**

Hunger scale: most people should try for a 3 before they eat and stop eating at 6.

Total Calories ( )

What I did today. What I need to improve. Actions I will take tomorrow.

Exercise _____ Duration _____ Calories Burned _____

Sleep Time to bed _____ Wake up _____ Hrs. _____ Min. _____

Date		M T W TH F S SU	Water ○ ○ ○ ○ ○ ○ ○ ○		
Time	Hunger rating before 1-10	FOOD		Hunger rating after 1-10	Calories

Hunger scale: most people should try for a 3 before they eat and stop eating at 6.

Total Calories ⬭

What I did today. What I need to improve. Actions I will take tomorrow.

Exercise _____ Duration _____ Calories Burned _____

Sleep Time to bed _____ Wake up _____ Hrs. _____ Min. _____

Date		M T W TH F S SU	Water ○ ○ ○ ○ ○ ○ ○		
Time	Hunger rating before 1-10	**FOOD**	Hunger rating after 1-10	**Calories**

Hunger scale: most people should try for a 3 before they eat and stop eating at 6.

Total Calories [   ]

What I did today. What I need to improve. Actions I will take tomorrow.

Exercise _____ Duration _____ Calories Burned _____

Sleep Time to bed _____ Wake up _____ Hrs. _____ Min. _____

Date		M T W TH F S SU	Water ◯ ◯ ◯ ◯ ◯ ◯ ◯	
Time	Hunger rating before 1-10	FOOD	Hunger rating after 1-10	Calories

Hunger scale: most people should try for a 3 before they eat and stop eating at 6.

Total Calories [   ]

What I did today. What I need to improve. Actions I will take tomorrow.

Exercise _____ Duration _____ Calories Burned _____

Sleep Time to bed _____ Wake up _____ Hrs. _____ Min._____

Date		M T W TH F S SU	Water ○ ○ ○ ○ ○ ○ ○ ○	
Time	Hunger rating before 1-10	**FOOD**	Hunger rating after 1-10	**Calories**

Hunger scale: most people should try for a 3 before they eat and stop eating at 6.

Total Calories ( )

What I did today. What I need to improve. Actions I will take tomorrow.

Exercise _____ Duration _____ Calories Burned _____

Sleep   Time to bed _____   Wake up _____   Hrs. _____   Min. _____

Date		M T W TH F S SU	Water ○ ○ ○ ○ ○ ○ ○ ○	
Time	**Hunger rating before 1-10**	**FOOD**	**Hunger rating after 1-10**	**Calories**

Hunger scale: most people should try for a 3 before they eat and stop eating at 6.

Total Calories [   ]

What I did today. What I need to improve. Actions I will take tomorrow.

Exercise _____ Duration _____ Calories Burned _____

Sleep Time to bed _____ Wake up _____ Hrs. _____ Min. _____

Date			M T W TH F S SU	Water ○ ○ ○ ○ ○ ○ ○		
Time	Hunger rating before 1-10	**FOOD**			Hunger rating after 1-10	**Calories**

Hunger scale: most people should try for a 3 before they eat and stop eating at 6.

Total Calories ( )

What I did today. What I need to improve. Actions I will take tomorrow.

Exercise _____ Duration _____ Calories Burned _____

Sleep   Time to bed _____   Wake up _____   Hrs. _____   Min. _____

Date		M T W TH F S SU	Water ◯ ◯ ◯ ◯ ◯ ◯ ◯		
Time	Hunger rating before **1-10**	**FOOD**	Hunger rating after **1-10**	**Calories**

Hunger scale: most people should try for a 3 before they eat and stop eating at 6.

Total Calories ⬭

What I did today. What I need to improve. Actions I will take tomorrow.

Exercise _____ Duration _____ Calories Burned _____

Sleep   Time to bed _____   Wake up _____   Hrs. _____   Min. _____

Time	Hunger rating before 1-10	FOOD	Hunger rating after 1-10	Calories

Date   M   T   W   TH   F   S   SU   **Water** ○ ○ ○ ○ ○ ○ ○ ○

Hunger scale: most people should try for a 3 before they eat and stop eating at 6.

Total Calories [ ]

What I did today. What I need to improve. Actions I will take tomorrow.

Exercise _____ Duration _____ Calories Burned _____

Sleep   Time to bed _____ Wake up _____ Hrs. _____ Min. _____

Date			M T W TH F S SU	Water ○ ○ ○ ○ ○ ○ ○ ○	
Time	Hunger rating before 1-10	FOOD		Hunger rating after 1-10	Calories

Hunger scale: most people should try for a 3 before they eat and stop eating at 6.

Total Calories ⬭

What I did today. What I need to improve. Actions I will take tomorrow.

Exercise _____ Duration _____ Calories Burned _____

Sleep Time to bed _____ Wake up _____ Hrs. _____ Min. _____

Date			M T W TH F S SU	Water ◯ ◯ ◯ ◯ ◯ ◯ ◯	
Time	Hunger rating before 1-10	FOOD		Hunger rating after 1-10	Calories

Hunger scale: most people should try for a 3 before they eat and stop eating at 6.

Total Calories

What I did today. What I need to improve. Actions I will take tomorrow.

Exercise _____ Duration _____ Calories Burned _____

Sleep   Time to bed _____   Wake up _____   Hrs. _____   Min. _____

Date		M T W TH F S SU	Water ○ ○ ○ ○ ○ ○ ○		
Time	Hunger rating before 1-10	**FOOD**		Hunger rating after 1-10	**Calories**

Hunger scale: most people should try for a 3 before they eat and stop eating at 6.

Total Calories [   ]

What I did today. What I need to improve. Actions I will take tomorrow.

Exercise _____ Duration _____ Calories Burned _____

Sleep   Time to bed _____ Wake up _____ Hrs. _____ Min. _____

Date			M T W TH F S SU	Water ○ ○ ○ ○ ○ ○ ○ ○		
Time	Hunger rating before 1-10		**FOOD**	Hunger rating after 1-10	**Calories**	

Hunger scale: most people should try for a 3 before they eat and stop eating at 6.

Total Calories ( )

What I did today. What I need to improve. Actions I will take tomorrow.

Exercise _____ Duration _____ Calories Burned _____

Sleep Time to bed _____ Wake up _____ Hrs. _____ Min. _____

Date		M T W TH F S SU	Water ○ ○ ○ ○ ○ ○ ○		
Time	Hunger rating before 1-10	**FOOD**	Hunger rating after 1-10	**Calories**

Hunger scale: most people should try for a 3 before they eat and stop eating at 6.

Total Calories ⬚

What I did today. What I need to improve. Actions I will take tomorrow.

Exercise _____ Duration _____ Calories Burned _____

Sleep   Time to bed _____ Wake up _____ Hrs. _____ Min. _____

Date		M T W TH F S SU	Water ○ ○ ○ ○ ○ ○ ○		
Time	Hunger rating before 1-10	**FOOD**	Hunger rating after 1-10	**Calories**

Hunger scale: most people should try for a 3 before they eat and stop eating at 6.

Total Calories ( )

What I did today. What I need to improve. Actions I will take tomorrow.

_____

_____

Exercise _____ Duration _____ Calories Burned _____

Sleep   Time to bed _____   Wake up _____   Hrs. _____   Min. _____

Date		M T W TH F S SU	Water ◯ ◯ ◯ ◯ ◯ ◯ ◯		
Time	Hunger rating before 1-10	FOOD	Hunger rating after 1-10	Calories

Hunger scale: most people should try for a 3 before they eat and stop eating at 6.   **Total Calories** ⬭

What I did today. What I need to improve. Actions I will take tomorrow.

Exercise _____ Duration _____ Calories Burned _____

Sleep   Time to bed _____ Wake up _____ Hrs. _____ Min. _____

Date		M T W TH F S SU	Water ○ ○ ○ ○ ○ ○ ○	
Time	Hunger rating before 1-10	FOOD	Hunger rating after 1-10	Calories

Hunger scale: most people should try for a 3 before they eat and stop eating at 6.

Total Calories ( )

What I did today. What I need to improve. Actions I will take tomorrow.

Exercise _____ Duration _____ Calories Burned _____

Sleep   Time to bed _____ Wake up _____ Hrs. _____ Min. _____

Date		M T W TH F S SU	Water ○ ○ ○ ○ ○ ○ ○ ○		
Time	Hunger rating before **1-10**	**FOOD**	Hunger rating after **1-10**	**Calories**

Hunger scale: most people should try for a 3 before they eat and stop eating at 6.

Total Calories ( )

What I did today. What I need to improve. Actions I will take tomorrow.

Exercise _____ Duration _____ Calories Burned _____

Sleep   Time to bed _____   Wake up _____   Hrs. _____   Min. _____

Date		M T W TH F S SU	Water ○ ○ ○ ○ ○ ○ ○	
Time	Hunger rating before 1-10	**FOOD**	Hunger rating after 1-10	**Calories**

Hunger scale: most people should try for a 3 before they eat and stop eating at 6.

Total Calories [   ]

What I did today. What I need to improve. Actions I will take tomorrow.

_____

_____

Exercise _____ Duration _____ Calories Burned _____

Sleep   Time to bed _____ Wake up _____ Hrs. _____ Min. _____

Date		M T W TH F S SU	Water ○ ○ ○ ○ ○ ○ ○	
Time	Hunger rating before 1-10	FOOD	Hunger rating after 1-10	Calories

Hunger scale: most people should try for a 3 before they eat and stop eating at 6.

Total Calories ( )

What I did today. What I need to improve. Actions I will take tomorrow.

Exercise _____ Duration _____ Calories Burned _____

Sleep Time to bed _____ Wake up _____ Hrs. _____ Min. _____

Date		M T W TH F S SU	Water ◯ ◯ ◯ ◯ ◯ ◯ ◯ ◯		
Time	Hunger rating before 1-10	**FOOD**	Hunger rating after 1-10	**Calories**

Hunger scale: most people should try for a 3 before they eat and stop eating at 6.

Total Calories ⬭

What I did today. What I need to improve. Actions I will take tomorrow.

Exercise _____ Duration _____ Calories Burned _____

Sleep Time to bed _____ Wake up _____ Hrs. _____ Min. _____

Date		M T W TH F S SU	Water ○ ○ ○ ○ ○ ○ ○ ○		
Time	Hunger rating before 1-10	FOOD		Hunger rating after 1-10	Calories

Hunger scale: most people should try for a 3 before they eat and stop eating at 6.

Total Calories (   )

What I did today. What I need to improve. Actions I will take tomorrow.

Exercise _____ Duration _____ Calories Burned _____

Sleep   Time to bed _____ Wake up _____ Hrs. _____ Min. _____

3rd Monthly Check-in

Date		M T W TH F S SU	Water ○ ○ ○ ○ ○ ○ ○ ○	
Time	Hunger rating before 1-10	FOOD	Hunger rating after 1-10	Calories

Hunger scale: most people should try for a 3 before they eat and stop eating at 6.

Total Calories ( )

What I did today. What I need to improve. Actions I will take tomorrow.

Exercise _____ Duration _____ Calories Burned _____

Sleep   Time to bed _____ Wake up _____ Hrs. _____ Min. _____

Date		M T W TH F S SU	Water ○ ○ ○ ○ ○ ○ ○		
Time	Hunger rating before 1-10	FOOD		Hunger rating after 1-10	Calories

Hunger scale: most people should try for a 3 before they eat and stop eating at 6.

Total Calories

What I did today. What I need to improve. Actions I will take tomorrow.

Exercise _____ Duration _____ Calories Burned _____

Sleep   Time to bed _____ Wake up _____ Hrs. _____ Min. _____

Date		M T W TH F S SU	Water ○ ○ ○ ○ ○ ○ ○	
Time	Hunger rating before 1-10	FOOD	Hunger rating after 1-10	Calories

Hunger scale: most people should try for a 3 before they eat and stop eating at 6.

Total Calories

What I did today. What I need to improve. Actions I will take tomorrow.

Exercise _____ Duration _____ Calories Burned _____

Sleep Time to bed _____ Wake up _____ Hrs. _____ Min. _____

Date			M T W TH F S SU	Water ◯ ◯ ◯ ◯ ◯ ◯ ◯ ◯	
Time	Hunger rating before 1-10	**FOOD**		Hunger rating after 1-10	**Calories**

Hunger scale: most people should try for a 3 before they eat and stop eating at 6.

Total Calories ( )

What I did today. What I need to improve. Actions I will take tomorrow.

Exercise _____ Duration _____ Calories Burned _____

Sleep   Time to bed _____   Wake up _____   Hrs. _____   Min. _____

Date		M T W TH F S SU	Water ◯ ◯ ◯ ◯ ◯ ◯ ◯ ◯		
Time	Hunger rating before 1-10	FOOD		Hunger rating after 1-10	Calories

Hunger scale: most people should try for a 3 before they eat and stop eating at 6.

Total Calories ⬭

What I did today. What I need to improve. Actions I will take tomorrow.

Exercise _____ Duration _____ Calories Burned _____

Sleep Time to bed _____ Wake up _____ Hrs. _____ Min. _____

Date		M T W TH F S SU	Water ○ ○ ○ ○ ○ ○ ○ ○	
Time	Hunger rating before 1-10	**FOOD**	Hunger rating after 1-10	**Calories**

Hunger scale: most people should try for a 3 before they eat and stop eating at 6.

Total Calories ⬭

What I did today. What I need to improve. Actions I will take tomorrow.

Exercise _____ Duration _____ Calories Burned _____

Sleep   Time to bed _____   Wake up _____   Hrs. _____   Min. _____

Date			M T W TH F S SU	Water ○ ○ ○ ○ ○ ○ ○ ○	
Time	Hunger rating before **1-10**	**FOOD**		Hunger rating after **1-10**	**Calories**

Hunger scale: most people should try for a 3 before they eat and stop eating at 6.

Total Calories ⬭

What I did today. What I need to improve. Actions I will take tomorrow.

Exercise _____ Duration _____ Calories Burned _____

Sleep Time to bed _____ Wake up _____ Hrs. _____ Min. _____

Date		M T W TH F S SU	Water ◯ ◯ ◯ ◯ ◯ ◯ ◯ ◯		
Time	Hunger rating before 1-10	FOOD		Hunger rating after 1-10	Calories

Hunger scale: most people should try for a 3 before they eat and stop eating at 6.

Total Calories ⟨____⟩

What I did today. What I need to improve. Actions I will take tomorrow.

Exercise _____ Duration _____ Calories Burned _____

Sleep Time to bed _____ Wake up _____ Hrs. _____ Min. _____

Date		M T W TH F S SU	Water ◯ ◯ ◯ ◯ ◯ ◯ ◯		
Time	Hunger rating before 1-10	FOOD		Hunger rating after 1-10	Calories

Hunger scale: most people should try for a 3 before they eat and stop eating at 6.

Total Calories

What I did today. What I need to improve. Actions I will take tomorrow.

Exercise _____ Duration _____ Calories Burned _____

Sleep   Time to bed _____ Wake up _____ Hrs. _____ Min. _____

Date		M T W TH F S SU	Water ○ ○ ○ ○ ○ ○ ○	
Time	Hunger rating before 1-10	**FOOD**	Hunger rating after 1-10	**Calories**

Hunger scale: most people should try for a 3 before they eat and stop eating at 6.

Total Calories ( )

What I did today. What I need to improve. Actions I will take tomorrow.

Exercise _____ Duration _____ Calories Burned _____

Sleep　Time to bed _____　Wake up _____　Hrs. _____　Min. _____

Date		M T W TH F S SU	Water ○ ○ ○ ○ ○ ○ ○		
Time	Hunger rating before 1-10	**FOOD**		Hunger rating after 1-10	**Calories**

Hunger scale: most people should try for a 3 before they eat and stop eating at 6.

Total Calories ⬭

What I did today. What I need to improve. Actions I will take tomorrow.

Exercise _____ Duration _____ Calories Burned _____

Sleep   Time to bed _____ Wake up _____ Hrs. _____ Min. _____

Date			M T W TH F S SU	Water ○ ○ ○ ○ ○ ○ ○	
Time	Hunger rating before 1-10	**FOOD**		Hunger rating after 1-10	**Calories**

Hunger scale: most people should try for a 3 before they eat and stop eating at 6.

Total Calories ⬭

What I did today. What I need to improve. Actions I will take tomorrow.

_____

_____

Exercise _____ Duration _____ Calories Burned _____

Sleep   Time to bed _____   Wake up _____   Hrs. _____   Min. _____

Date		M T W TH F S SU	Water ○ ○ ○ ○ ○ ○ ○ ○		
Time	Hunger rating before 1-10	FOOD	Hunger rating after 1-10	Calories

Hunger scale: most people should try for a 3 before they eat and stop eating at 6.

Total Calories ⬡

What I did today. What I need to improve. Actions I will take tomorrow.

Exercise _____ Duration _____ Calories Burned _____

Sleep   Time to bed _____ Wake up _____ Hrs. _____ Min. _____

Date		M T W TH F S SU	Water ○ ○ ○ ○ ○ ○ ○	
Time	Hunger rating before 1-10	**FOOD**	Hunger rating after 1-10	**Calories**

Hunger scale: most people should try for a 3 before they eat and stop eating at 6.

Total Calories ( )

What I did today. What I need to improve. Actions I will take tomorrow.

Exercise _____ Duration _____ Calories Burned _____

Sleep Time to bed _____ Wake up _____ Hrs. _____ Min. _____

Date		M T W TH F S SU	Water ○ ○ ○ ○ ○ ○ ○ ○		
Time	Hunger rating before 1-10	**FOOD**		Hunger rating after 1-10	**Calories**

Hunger scale: most people should try for a 3 before they eat and stop eating at 6.

Total Calories ⬚

What I did today. What I need to improve. Actions I will take tomorrow.

Exercise _____ Duration _____ Calories Burned _____

Sleep Time to bed _____ Wake up _____ Hrs. _____ Min. _____

Date		M T W TH F S SU	Water ○ ○ ○ ○ ○ ○ ○ ○		
Time	Hunger rating before 1-10	FOOD	Hunger rating after 1-10	Calories

Hunger scale: most people should try for a 3 before they eat and stop eating at 6.

Total Calories ( )

What I did today. What I need to improve. Actions I will take tomorrow.

Exercise _____ Duration _____ Calories Burned _____

Sleep   Time to bed _____ Wake up _____ Hrs. _____ Min. _____

Date		M T W TH F S SU	Water ○ ○ ○ ○ ○ ○ ○		
Time	Hunger rating before 1-10	FOOD		Hunger rating after 1-10	Calories

Hunger scale: most people should try for a 3 before they eat and stop eating at 6.

Total Calories [   ]

What I did today. What I need to improve. Actions I will take tomorrow.

_____

_____

Exercise _____ Duration _____ Calories Burned _____

Sleep   Time to bed _____ Wake up _____ Hrs. _____ Min. _____

121

Date		M T W TH F S SU	Water ○ ○ ○ ○ ○ ○ ○ ○		
Time	Hunger rating before 1-10	FOOD		Hunger rating after 1-10	Calories

Hunger scale: most people should try for a 3 before they eat and stop eating at 6.

Total Calories

Calories

What I did today. What I need to improve. Actions I will take tomorrow.

Exercise _____ Duration _____ Calories Burned _____

Sleep   Time to bed _____   Wake up _____   Hrs. _____   Min. _____

Date		M T W TH F S SU	Water ○ ○ ○ ○ ○ ○ ○ ○		
Time	Hunger rating before 1-10	FOOD		Hunger rating after 1-10	Calories

Hunger scale: most people should try for a 3 before they eat and stop eating at 6.

Total Calories [   ]

What I did today. What I need to improve. Actions I will take tomorrow.

_____

_____

Exercise _____ Duration _____ Calories Burned _____

Sleep   Time to bed _____ Wake up _____ Hrs. _____ Min. _____

Date		M T W TH F S SU	Water ○ ○ ○ ○ ○ ○ ○		
Time	Hunger rating before 1-10	FOOD	Hunger rating after 1-10	Calories

Hunger scale: most people should try for a 3 before they eat and stop eating at 6.

Total Calories [   ]

What I did today. What I need to improve. Actions I will take tomorrow.

Exercise _____ Duration _____ Calories Burned _____

Sleep Time to bed _____ Wake up _____ Hrs. _____ Min. _____

Date		M T W TH F S SU	Water ○ ○ ○ ○ ○ ○ ○	
Time	Hunger rating before 1-10	**FOOD**	Hunger rating after 1-10	**Calories**

Hunger scale: most people should try for a 3 before they eat and stop eating at 6.

Total Calories [   ]

What I did today. What I need to improve. Actions I will take tomorrow.

Exercise _____ Duration _____ Calories Burned _____

Sleep   Time to bed _____ Wake up _____ Hrs. _____ Min. _____

Date		M T W TH F S SU	Water ○ ○ ○ ○ ○ ○ ○		
Time	Hunger rating before 1-10	FOOD	Hunger rating after 1-10	Calories

Hunger scale: most people should try for a 3 before they eat and stop eating at 6.

Total Calories [   ]

What I did today. What I need to improve. Actions I will take tomorrow.

Exercise _____ Duration _____ Calories Burned _____

Sleep Time to bed _____ Wake up _____ Hrs. _____ Min. _____

Date		M T W TH F S SU	Water ○ ○ ○ ○ ○ ○ ○ ○		
Time	Hunger rating before 1-10	**FOOD**		Hunger rating after 1-10	**Calories**

Hunger scale: most people should try for a 3 before they eat and stop eating at 6.

Total Calories ( )

What I did today. What I need to improve. Actions I will take tomorrow.

Exercise _____ Duration _____ Calories Burned _____

Sleep Time to bed _____ Wake up _____ Hrs. _____ Min. _____

Date		M T W TH F S SU	Water ○ ○ ○ ○ ○ ○ ○

Time	Hunger rating before 1-10	FOOD	Hunger rating after 1-10	Calories

Hunger scale: most people should try for a 3 before they eat and stop eating at 6.

Total Calories ⬭

What I did today. What I need to improve. Actions I will take tomorrow.

Exercise _____ Duration _____ Calories Burned _____

Sleep Time to bed _____ Wake up _____ Hrs. _____ Min. _____

Date		M T W TH F S SU	Water ○ ○ ○ ○ ○ ○ ○ ○		
Time	**Hunger rating before 1-10**	**FOOD**		**Hunger rating after 1-10**	**Calories**

Hunger scale: most people should try for a 3 before they eat and stop eating at 6.

Total Calories ( )

What I did today. What I need to improve. Actions I will take tomorrow.

Exercise _____ Duration _____ Calories Burned _____

Sleep Time to bed _____ Wake up _____ Hrs. _____ Min. _____

Date		M T W TH F S SU	Water ○ ○ ○ ○ ○ ○ ○ ○		
Time	Hunger rating before 1-10	**FOOD**	Hunger rating after 1-10	**Calories**	

Hunger scale: most people should try for a 3 before they eat and stop eating at 6.

Total Calories ( )

What I did today. What I need to improve. Actions I will take tomorrow.

Exercise _____ Duration _____ Calories Burned _____

Sleep Time to bed _____ Wake up _____ Hrs. _____ Min. _____

Date		M T W TH F S SU	Water ○ ○ ○ ○ ○ ○ ○ ○	
Time	Hunger rating before 1-10	**FOOD**	Hunger rating after 1-10	**Calories**

Hunger scale: most people should try for a 3 before they eat and stop eating at 6.

Total Calories

What I did today. What I need to improve. Actions I will take tomorrow.

Exercise _____ Duration _____ Calories Burned _____

Sleep   Time to bed _____ Wake up _____ Hrs. _____ Min. _____

Date		M T W TH F S SU	Water ○ ○ ○ ○ ○ ○ ○		
Time	Hunger rating before 1-10	**FOOD**		Hunger rating after 1-10	**Calories**

Hunger scale: most people should try for a 3 before they eat and stop eating at 6.

Total Calories ( )

What I did today. What I need to improve. Actions I will take tomorrow.

Exercise _____ Duration _____ Calories Burned _____

Sleep Time to bed _____ Wake up _____ Hrs. _____ Min. _____

Date		M T W TH F S SU	Water ○ ○ ○ ○ ○ ○ ○		
Time	Hunger rating before 1-10	FOOD		Hunger rating after 1-10	Calories

Hunger scale: most people should try for a 3 before they eat and stop eating at 6.

Total Calories ⬭

What I did today. What I need to improve. Actions I will take tomorrow.

_____

_____

Exercise _____ Duration _____ Calories Burned _____

Sleep   Time to bed _____ Wake up _____ Hrs. _____ Min. _____

Date		M T W TH F S SU **Water** ○ ○ ○ ○ ○ ○ ○ ○		
Time	Hunger rating before 1-10	**FOOD**	Hunger rating after 1-10	**Calories**

Hunger scale: most people should try for a 3 before they eat and stop eating at 6.

Total Calories ( )

What I did today. What I need to improve. Actions I will take tomorrow.

Exercise _____ Duration _____ Calories Burned _____

Sleep   Time to bed _____   Wake up _____   Hrs. _____   Min. _____

Date		M T W TH F S SU	**Water** ○ ○ ○ ○ ○ ○ ○ ○	
Time	Hunger rating before 1-10	**FOOD**	Hunger rating after 1-10	**Calories**

Hunger scale: most people should try for a 3 before they eat and stop eating at 6.

Total Calories ( )

What I did today. What I need to improve. Actions I will take tomorrow.

Exercise _____ Duration _____ Calories Burned _____

Sleep Time to bed _____ Wake up _____ Hrs. _____ Min. _____

4th Monthly Check-in

Calories for my common foods

Cheerios, 1 cup — 100 calories

Another Journal by Design Your Life:

Weekly Meal Planner with Grocery Ideas
Save Money, Save Time, Eat Healthy

Made in the USA
Coppell, TX
29 August 2021